Mid-America $18.95 Lexile: 750

4/18

AMERICAN GIRL ENTREPRENEUR

Pleasant Rowland

PAIGE V. POLINSKY

**Checkerboard
Library**

An Imprint of Abdo Publishing
abdopublishing.com

abdopublishing.com

Printed in the United States of America, North Mankato, Minnesota
062017
092017

 THIS BOOK CONTAINS
RECYCLED MATERIALS

Design and Production: Mighty Media, Inc.
Editor: Liz Salzmann
Cover Photographs: John Maniaci/Wisconsin State Journal/State Journal Archive (center); Mighty Media, Inc. (border)
Interior Photographs: Alamy, pp. 11, 15, 29 (bottom left); AP Images, p. 19; Courtesy of The Strong®, Rochester, New York, pp. 13, 17, 23, 28 (right); iStockphoto, pp. 8, 20, 29 (top); John Maniaci/Wisconsin State Journal/State Journal Archive, p. 16; Paul Malo/Wikimedia Commons, p. 24; Seth Poppel/Yearbook Library, p. 5; Shutterstock, pp. 7, 9, 21, 22, 28 (left), 29 (bottom right)

Publisher's Cataloging-in-Publication Data
Names: Polinsky, Paige V., author.
Title: American Girl entrepreneur: Pleasant Rowland / by Paige V. Polinsky.
Other titles: Pleasant Rowland
Description: Minneapolis, MN : Abdo Publishing, 2018. | Series: Toy trailblazers |
    Includes bibliographical references and index.
Identifiers: LCCN 2016962798 | ISBN 9781532110948 (lib. bdg.) |
    ISBN 9781680788792 (ebook)
Subjects: LCSH: Rowland, Pleasant, 1942- --Juvenile literature. | American Girl
    (Firm)--Juvenile literature. | Dollmakers--United States--Biography--Juvenile
    literature. | Toymakers--United States--Biography--Juvenile literature.
Classification: DDC 745.592/092 [B]--dc23
LC record available at http://lccn.loc.gov/2016962798

CONTENTS

Chapter 1

Born to TEACH

Pleasant Rowland was born in Chicago, Illinois, in 1941. She had three younger sisters and a younger brother. Pleasant's father ran a successful advertising agency. Growing up, Pleasant saw her father's **marketing** ideas turn into realities. He taught her the importance of patience and paying careful attention to details. Pleasant would later use these skills to create the famous American Girl dolls.

As a child, Pleasant loved reading and going to school. She wanted to be a teacher when she grew up. In 1958, Rowland attended Wells College in Aurora, New York. Wells was a small private school for women. Rowland studied English there. After graduating in 1962, she moved to Massachusetts. She began teaching first and second graders at a school in Mattapan.

Rowland was living her childhood dream. But she was disappointed with the resources **available** for teachers. Reading lessons were difficult and boring. Her students were

FUN FACT

Wells College started admitting male students in 2005.

struggling. So, Rowland got to work. After a lot of research, Rowland created a special system to teach reading. She wrote the materials herself. When she became a kindergarten teacher, she adjusted this system for her younger students. It was a tremendous success.

Rowland once said, "Reading is at the heart of all achievement. Without it, the American dream is out of reach. With it, anything is possible."

Chapter 2

TEXTBOOK
Titan

Rowland loved helping children learn. But in 1968, she decided to try something new. That year, she applied for a job at a TV station. She began working as a reporter in San Francisco, California. Rowland was eventually promoted to news anchor. It was a fun job. But Rowland wanted to make a difference in people's lives. After three years, she was ready for another change. So, she returned to the world of education.

Rowland gathered the materials she had created while teaching. She turned them into a teacher's guide. *Beginning to Read, Write and Listen* was published in 1971. The textbook became very popular. It was the first organized system created to teach kindergarteners reading and writing. Rowland published other textbooks over the next few years.

In 1977, Rowland married Jerry Frautschi. They settled in Madison, Wisconsin. Frautschi owned a book-printing company there. In Madison, Rowland dedicated herself to writing and volunteer work. In 1981, she bought the company that published the *Children's Magazine Guide*.

Frautschi's family has lived in the Madison area since the 1860s! They have donated millions of dollars to develop the city and expand art and education programs.

This was a library resource for **elementary school** children. Rowland's leadership boosted the guide's sales **dramatically**. It was clear she had talent for business!

Chapter 3

A Life-Changing TRIP

In 1984, Rowland and Frautschi visited Williamsburg, Virginia. There, Rowland explored Colonial Williamsburg. The living history museum there was much more interesting than a school textbook. Rowland wished that all children could learn about history in this exciting way.

That Christmas, Rowland went shopping for her nieces. Rowland knew that they both wanted dolls for Christmas. But she was unimpressed with the dolls she found. Many of them encouraged girls to be make-believe mothers. Others focused on children's future careers. Rowland wanted dolls that simply let girls be girls.

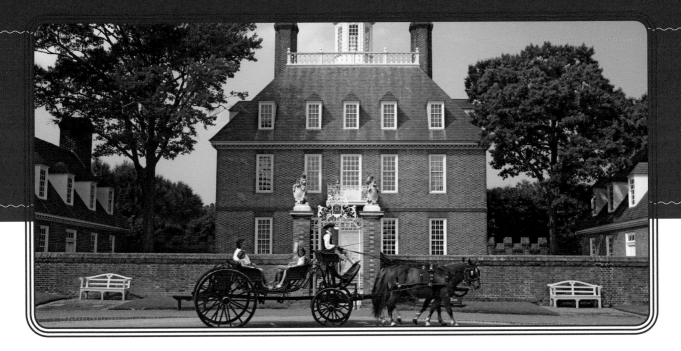

Colonial Williamsburg is the historic district of Williamsburg, Virginia. It is a living history museum where people dress up in costumes and act out scenes from Colonial life!

While shopping, Rowland recalled her visit to Williamsburg. She suddenly had an idea. What if she created dolls of her own? Each doll could belong to a different historic period. And each doll could come with a book. Girls could read about history through their dolls' adventures!

A few months later, Rowland and her husband spent a weekend at their cabin in northern Wisconsin. Rowland spent the entire time writing. She created characters and designed clothing. Soon she had a complete business plan. In 1986, Rowland used profits from her textbook sales to start the Pleasant Company.

Chapter 4

Bumpy BEGINNING

Rowland worked with her friend Valerie Tripp. Tripp was a children's author. They created three historical characters. One was Samantha, an orphan adopted by her wealthy grandmother in 1904. The second was Molly, who lived in 1944 during **World War II**. The third was Kirsten, a Swedish **immigrant** living on the American frontier in 1854.

These characters were called American Girls. Tripp wrote a set of six books for each character. Then they designed a doll for each American Girl. Rowland had plenty of story and character ideas for the American Girl books. But she didn't know how to create a doll from scratch. So, she tried to find a usable example to start with. She enlisted a friend to help. The friend found an old German doll in a Chicago second-hand store. Rowland loved the doll's design. She used it as a model for her dolls.

FUN FACT

Rowland chose the first dolls' fabrics and ribbons herself.

Molly and Kirsten were retired in 2009 and are no longer for sale. Samantha was initially retired but was brought back in 2014 with new clothes and accessories!

Rowland hired the same German doll company to make her American Girl dolls. She hired a Chinese company to produce their **accessories**. Meanwhile, the Pleasant Company published the American Girl books. It wasn't very **glamorous** work. Rowland and her employees worked from an old warehouse in Madison. They used **plywood** and old doors to build their packing stations. The building's heat didn't work. The doll-making business was proving to be tough work.

Chapter 5

DOUBT
and Determination

A cold factory was the least of Rowland's worries. She also dealt with plenty of criticism. Many people said her dolls would fail. They thought the historical themes would be too boring. And they thought **marketing** the dolls to girls between 7 and 12 years old would be difficult. They didn't think girls that age would be interested in dolls. But Rowland trusted her instincts. She remained **confident** in her idea.

Rowland knew that American Girl dolls could be a hit. But they would only succeed with proper marketing. The books and dolls were not loud and flashy like many electronic toys on the market at the time. They would not stand out on a store **shelf** or in a TV commercial. And because of their high quality, they were much more expensive than most other dolls. Many stores didn't want to sell them. So, Rowland decided to advertise

FUN FACT

Even the mailing list company doubted Rowland's success. They encouraged her to send only 100,000 catalogs.

American Girl dolls cost $115. This includes the doll, her outfit, and a book featuring the character.

Rebecca

American Girl products in special catalogs.

In September 1986, the Pleasant Company mailed catalogs to 500,000 homes around the country. The catalogs advertised the American Girl products for sale. Interested customers could mail their orders directly to the company. And there were plenty of interested customers. By December 31, the Pleasant Company had earned $1.7 million in sales!

Chapter 6

Preteen POWER

Rowland's critics had been wrong. The American Girl dolls were a major success! The Pleasant Company was reaching out to a group that had been forgotten by most toymakers. For the first time, preteen girls were being treated as valued customers. The American Girl stories told girls that they mattered.

American Girl dolls were popular with parents too. The American Girl characters were in no rush to grow up. They looked and acted like young girls instead of imitating adult roles. And on top of that, they were educational! By blending history with playtime, Rowland had created something truly special.

The American Girl books were another reason for Rowland's success. Girls fell in love with Samantha, Molly, and Kirsten while reading their stories. They wanted the doll **versions** of the characters they loved. Then, they also wanted the clothes, furniture, and **accessories** to go with the dolls. Rowland's business grew quickly.

In 1989, the Pleasant Company moved its headquarters to Middleton, Wisconsin. Rowland's success was very exciting. But that same year, she faced a brand-new challenge. She was **diagnosed** with breast **cancer**. Rowland underwent surgery and **chemotherapy**. It was exhausting. But working kept her spirits high. Rowland was proud of her company's success. And thankfully, her cancer eventually went into **remission**.

The American Girl dolls were so successful that the company started making dolls of the main characters' best friends!

Chapter 7

Growing UP

The American Girl brand kept growing. During the 1990s, three new historical dolls were added to the collection. And in 1992, Rowland started *American Girl* magazine. It was published six times per year. At first, the magazine promoted the company's products. It also included short stories about the different characters. Over time, the magazine grew to focus less on the dolls and more on the girls playing with them. Today, it features crafts, recipes, advice, and more.

In 1988, the Pleasant Company opened an American Girl doll hospital. Girls can send broken American Girl dolls to this hospital be fixed. There,

American Girl introduced the Bitty Baby line of dolls in 1995. These smaller baby dolls were meant for younger children.

special toy makers called doll doctors make the dolls good as new. Since 1992, each doll is sent home with a hospital gown and bracelet. She also carries a **certificate** of good health and a get-well balloon!

In 1995, the Pleasant Company released a new line of American Girl dolls. The dolls came in a **variety** of hair, skin, and eye colors. The line was called American Girl of Today. These dolls were not from specific historical eras. Instead, girls could create the stories themselves!

American Girl of Today dolls come with blank Friends Forever notebooks. In them, girls can write their dolls' stories.

Chapter 8

Where the Magic HAPPENS

The American Girl headquarters are still located in Middleton. New historical and Girl of the Year characters are constantly being developed there. Each new American Girl doll goes through an **intense** research and design process.

First, the researchers choose a place and historical period for the character. They spend the next three years learning about the selected time period. They study the area's **culture**, geography, **cuisine**, and more. They consult museum **curators**, **linguists**, and other professionals for help. The researchers travel to the real-life city chosen as the character's hometown to learn more about it.

This research does more than shape the character's story. It also creates her look. Researchers help designers choose the doll's clothing and hairstyle. Sometimes they call in experts. For example, members of the Nez Perce tribe helped develop Kaya, a Native American character. They made sure that Kaya's face, braids, and outfit patterns were **authentic**.

EYES

American Girl dolls' eyes and eyelids are painted by hand. Then the eyelashes are attached to the eyes.

HAIR

American Girl dolls have wigged hair. This means the fibers are sewn onto a wig cap. The cap is then glued onto the doll's head.

HEADS AND LIMBS

The American Girl factory uses molds to make the dolls' heads and limbs. Melted vinyl is poured into each mold. The molds then spin very quickly. The force of the spin causes the vinyl to spread evenly throughout the molds. The material is then cooled. This process is called spin casting.

BODIES

The dolls are put together by workers on an assembly line. The dolls' cloth bodies are sewn and stuffed by hand. The arms and legs are sewn to the body. A hidden neck cord attaches the head to the body.

Chapter 9

Company SALE

By 1998, American Girl products were earning $300 million each year. Rowland was proud of her American Girl empire. She knew that she had done her very best to grow the business and make it special. But she was finally ready to pass that job on to someone else.

She found the perfect someone in Jill Barad, the CEO of Mattel toy company. Rowland was impressed with Barad's work **marketing** the world-famous Barbie doll. In 1998, Rowland sold her company to Mattel for more than $700 million.

The American Girl Collection continued to flourish after the sale. In 2001, Mattel released the first American Girl of the Year. Like the historical dolls, this character came with her own

FUN FACT

In 2004, the first American Girl movie was released. *An American Girl Holiday* followed Samantha's story. There are now 12 American Girl movies.

Mattel is the largest toy manufacturer in the world! Besides American Girl, it is known for making Barbie dolls, Hot Wheels cars, and more.

books and backstory. But she was from the present day. Her challenges and **accessories** were modern.

Under Mattel, the American Girl of Today line was renamed the Truly Me line. Mattel focused on the modern Truly Me dolls more than the brand's classic, historical dolls. Some American Girl fans were disappointed in this shift. They liked the historical dolls. But Truly Me helped the American Girl brand stay modern and **relevant**. Girls could now buy items such as tiny headphones and laptops. Their dolls could be just like them!

Chapter 10

Giving BACK

Rowland stayed busy after selling American Girl. The American Girl collection had made her extremely wealthy. She wanted to use the money to help others. In 1998, she created the Pleasant T. Rowland Foundation. It supports many art and education projects.

Rowland's idea for the foundation was largely inspired by her husband. Frautschi came from a very wealthy family. His relatives were known throughout Wisconsin for giving back to the community. Rowland wanted to do the same.

Rowland received an honorary degree from the University of Wisconsin–Madison for her business and charitable achievements!

In 1997, the Learning Company developed an American Girl computer game. In the game, girls can create plays featuring the historical American Girl characters.

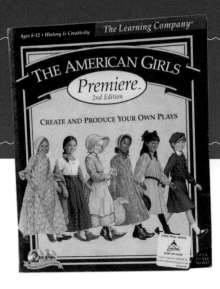

The Pleasant T. Rowland Foundation funded the creation of a visitor's center at Ten Chimneys. This is a theatrical arts museum in Wisconsin. It also funded the expansion of the Waisman Early Childhood Program at the University of Wisconsin–Madison. Waisman's programs promote the education of children with disabilities.

In 2003, Rowland again returned to education. She wanted children to be excited to learn new things. And she remembered the difficulties in finding high-quality teaching materials. So, in 2003, she started the Rowland Reading Foundation. It provides teachers with extra training and resources to help their students read better.

FUN FACT

In the late 1990s, Rowland and Frautschi **donated** $205 million to build the Overture Center for the Arts in Madison. It is one of the largest single donations to the arts in American history.

Chapter 11

The Aurora
FOUNDATION

Rowland has **donated** to many different projects over the years. But the Aurora Foundation is one of her most well-known efforts. In the late 1990s, Rowland was contacted by Wells College president Lisa Ryerson.

Ryerson was looking for someone willing to make a large donation to **renovate**

The Aurora Inn, built in 1833, was closed several times due to financial troubles before Rowland's renovations. It has received rave reviews from visitors since reopening in 2003.

some buildings in and around the campus. The population of Aurora, the town where the college is located, was **declining**. With fewer people to care for them, some of the historic buildings were in bad shape.

Ryerson hoped Rowland cared enough about the school to help out. Rowland did care, and was excited to give back to the school she loved so much. She lost no time in creating the Aurora Foundation. It planned to change Aurora back to the way Rowland remembered it.

The restoration plans were finalized and presented in 2001. Rowland played a huge role in the project. She paid careful attention to the details. Aurora was beautiful by the time Rowland was done. Six buildings and two homes were fully restored. Some of the town's members were not as excited as Rowland. They felt that she was changing the town too much. But many were delighted by the transformation.

Chapter 12

THE MODERN
American Girl

Pleasant Rowland showed determination in everything she did. She created a successful business and many well-known foundations. Her hard work to bring her American Girl idea to life sparked a toy sensation. More than 29 million American Girl dolls have been sold since their release.

Mattel continues to produce exciting new products. Today there are 40 different Truly Me dolls **available**. But Rowland's original vision has not been forgotten.

In 2014, the historical American Girl dolls were given a fresh new look. They were renamed the BeForever dolls. Their books, outfits, and **accessories** were updated. And in 2016, the world met a new BeForever doll. Melody is a girl growing up during the civil rights movement of the 1960s.

Rowland is pleased with Mattel's work on American Girl. While her toy **legacy** continues without her, she focuses on the Rowland Reading Foundation. In 2009, she entered the Association of Educational

There are 20 American Girl retail stores. They have received more than 80 million visitors!

Publishers' Hall of Fame. But the fame and fortune has not gone to her head. Today, Pleasant Rowland leads a quiet, private life in Madison.

TIMELINE

1941
Pleasant Rowland is born in Chicago, Illinois.

1977
Rowland marries Jerry Frautschi. They settle in Madison, Wisconsin.

1962
Rowland graduates from Wells College in Aurora, New York.

1971
Rowland publishes her first textbook.

1984
Rowland visits Williamsburg, Virginia. She gets the idea for the American Girl dolls.

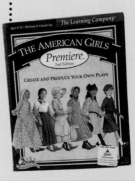

American Girl is known for blending education and playtime together. Rowland calls this approach "chocolate cake with vitamins."

1986

Rowland starts the Pleasant Company. The first American Girl dolls are sold.

1992

Rowland starts *American Girl* magazine.

2009

Rowland enters the Association of Educational Publishers' Hall of Fame.

1995

The Pleasant Company introduces the American Girl of Today dolls.

1998

Rowland sells the Pleasant Company to Mattel.

Glossary

accessory – an optional part that adds to the beauty, convenience, or effectiveness of something.

authentic – real.

available – able to be had or used.

cancer – any of a group of often deadly diseases marked by harmful changes in the normal growth of cells. Cancer can spread and destroy healthy tissues and organs.

certificate – a paper that says someone has fulfilled certain requirements.

chemotherapy – the use of chemicals to treat a disease such as cancer.

confident – sure of oneself.

cuisine (kwih-ZEEN) – a way or style of cooking food.

culture – the customs, arts, and tools of a nation or a people at a certain time.

curator – a person in charge of a museum or a zoo.

decline – to tend toward an inferior state or a weaker condition.

diagnose – to recognize something, such as a disease, by signs, symptoms, or tests.

donate – to give. A donation is something that is given.

dramatically – very noticeably.

elementary school – a school that children attend from kindergarten through fifth or sixth grade.

glamorous – beautiful and exciting.

WEBSITES

To learn more about Toy Trailblazers, visit **abdobooklinks.com**. These links are routinely monitored and updated to provide the most current information available.

immigrant – a person who enters another country to live.

intense – marked by great energy, determination, or concentration.

legacy – something important or meaningful handed down from previous generations or from the past.

linguist – a person who studies human speech and language.

marketing – the activities done to make buyers aware of and want to buy a service or product.

plywood – large, flat boards made with layers of wood glued together.

relevant – related to one's knowledge and experience.

remission – a state or period during which the symptoms of a disease are lessened.

renovate – to restore by rebuilding or repairing.

shelf – a thin, flat surface used to store things.

variety – different types of one thing.

version – a different form or type of an original.

World War II – from 1939 to 1945, fought in Europe, Asia, and Africa. Great Britain, France, the United States, the Soviet Union, and their allies were on one side. Germany, Italy, Japan, and their allies were on the other side.

Index